# CREATIVITY DOT AI

**Empowering Your Creativity in a World
Transformed by AI**

DA SACHIN SHARMA

*This book is dedicated to my beloved wife, Vidhi Angira, my daughter, the talented writer Da Sashyavi Sharma, and my parents, Poonam Chandra Sharma and Varsha Sharma, thank you for helping shape me into the person I am today*

# Contents

*"What you know today*
*may not be what you need to know*
*tomorrow*
*be ready to unlearn"*


*- da sachin sharma*

Preface

As the world continues to evolve and technology continues to advance, it is becoming increasingly important for creative professionals to stay ahead of the curve. The introduction of Artificial Intelligence (AI) has revolutionized the way in which many industries operate, and the creative field is no exception.

While AI has the potential to automate certain aspects of the creative process, it also presents new opportunities for growth and innovation. However, many creative professionals remain sceptical of AI, uncertain of its impact on their field and how to incorporate AI into their work.

In this book, I aim to educate creative professionals on the benefits and challenges of incorporating AI into their work, and provide practical tips and exercises for doing so. Through storytelling and the use of industry quotes, I hope to provide a comprehensive and accessible look at the current state of AI in the creative field.

By embracing AI and incorporating it into their work, creative professionals can stay ahead of the curve, continue to innovate and grow, and ensure that their skills and expertise remain valuable in an ever-changing landscape.

This book is for anyone who is interested in the intersection of AI and creativity, and wants to understand how they can adapt and thrive in the era of AI. I believe that by embracing the change that AI represents, we can continue to push the boundaries of creativity and bring new and exciting ideas to the world.

## Acknowledgments

It is with great gratitude that I acknowledge the individuals who have been instrumental in bringing this book to life.

First and foremost, I would like to thank my parents for instilling in me the belief that I can live my life to the fullest. Their words "ja beta jeele apni zindagi" have always been a source of motivation for me.

I would like to express my heartfelt thanks to Abhishek Porwal and Vishal Gupta, who are not only my business partners but also my friends and family. They have always been there for me, providing me with the support and encouragement I needed to pursue my knowledge and ideas.

I am grateful to the Co-founders of Mobilla, Dr. Jignesh Shah and Hetal Shah, for providing me with the opportunity to work with such an amazing brand and for encouraging me to bring my knowledge to the brand's day-to-day marketing initiatives.

Finally, I would like to extend my deepest appreciation to my wife, Vidhi Angira, for being my constant source of support and inspiration. Her unwavering belief in my abilities and her daily motivation has been the driving force behind my creative pursuits.

Special thanks to Puneet Bhatnagar, who has given me the extra push I needed to pursue my passion and to keep doing and publishing my research on AI.

Last but not least, I would like to acknowledge my editor Harshita, who was there for me at the last minute and provided me with the support I needed to publish this book. Thank you, Harshita, for your tireless efforts and for being such an important part of this project.

Thank you, everyone, for being a part of this journey and for supporting me in every step of the way. I hope this book will inspire and empower creativity in the world of AI.

Prologue

## The Rise of AI and the Future of Creativity

Hello readers! I am the author of this book and I want to share with you my thoughts behind it. As we all know, the world is changing rapidly and technology is at the forefront of that change. One of the most impactful technologies is Artificial Intelligence, which has been making waves in various industries and creative fields are no exception. As a creative professional myself, I have seen the impact of AI on my own work and the work of others in my community. This is why I felt compelled to write this book - to educate and inform the creative fraternity about the changes brought about by AI, and to encourage them to embrace and adapt to this change.

I understand that the topic of AI can be intimidating, so I have tried to make the content of this book as approachable and relatable as possible. Throughout the book, I have included stories and quotes to help illustrate the concepts and make them easier to understand.

Additionally, I have made sure to use simple language, so that readers with any level of technical knowledge can follow along.

My goal is to not only educate creative professionals about AI, but also to inspire them to see the opportunities that this technology presents. I truly believe that, with the right mindset and approach, AI can be a powerful tool for enhancing and expanding creativity, rather than limiting it. I hope that, by the end of this book, you will feel more confident and equipped to navigate the AI-driven creative landscape.

So, let's get started on this journey of exploring the impact of AI on creativity, and how we can use it to shape a brighter future for our industry.

*"The illiterate of the 21st century will not be those who cannot read and write, but those who cannot learn, unlearn, and relearn."*

# CHAPTER ONE

# The History

The launch of the first computer in the 1970s marked the beginning of a technological revolution that changed the world as we know it. Those who adapted to the change, learned the new technology and embraced it, survived and thrived in the ever-changing business landscape. On the other hand, those who refused to adapt, who stuck to the traditional methods, soon found themselves out of business. The same scenario is playing out once again with the introduction of AI and machine learning.

Bill Gates and Steve Jobs, two of the biggest names in the tech industry, have often talked about the impact of computers on the world. Bill Gates said, "The computer was born to solve problems that did not exist before." Steve Jobs, on the other hand, said, "Computers themselves, and software yet to be developed, will revolutionize the way we learn." Both of these statements have proven to be true, as computers have transformed the way we live, work, and communicate.

Fast forward to the present, and we are witnessing a similar revolution with the advent of AI and machine learning. The launch of OpenAI's GPT-3 and Stable Diffusion's MidJourney has created a stir in the creative industry. These AI-powered systems have the ability to create high-quality content, design graphics and illustrations, and even write stories and scripts. This has made them a threat to the traditional creative professionals. However, it is not the time to resist the change. It is the time to embrace it.

As the CEO of Stable Diffusion, Jean-François Gagné, says, "The future belongs to those who understand and embrace the power of technology. It is time for creative professionals to take control of their own future, to use AI as a tool to enhance their skills and produce even better work." This book is about educating the creative fraternity about the rise of AI, its impact on the industry, and how to embrace the change and move with time.

Through simple language, stories, and quotes, I aim to help creative professionals understand the benefits of AI, and how it can be used to enhance their skills and produce even better work. This book is a call to action, to urge creative professionals to adapt, to learn, and to use AI as a tool for their growth and success. The time is now to shape the future of AI and creativity.

# CHAPTER TWO

# The Current State of AI

*AI has been proven to help us make more meaningful*
*connections between different concepts.*

–   *-Mark Zuckerberg, CEO of Facebook*

Artificial Intelligence (AI) has been in the public eye for a while now, with some heralding it as the greatest technological advancement of our time and others warning us of its potential dangers. But what does AI mean for the creative industry?

AI is undeniably shaking things up in the creative sector, changing how artists and professionals collaborate and create. It's being used to automate mundane tasks, freeing up creatives to focus on work of greater importance, while also providing new tools to allow them to push boundaries even further.

However, every technology comes with both benefits and drawbacks—and AI is no exception here. While it can help streamline processes or provide neat features that weren't available before, it can also take away jobs from creative professionals.

"AI has proven to be a great companion for creatives, both in the development of ideas and their implementation" says Danny Dang, CEO of a London-based production company. "It's allowed us to produce higher quality work that would have otherwise taken significantly more time and resources with conventional techniques."

This efficiency is one of the key benefits AI technologies can provide in the creative sector—but it's not the only one. With AI-powered tools like natural language processing and image recognition being applied to everything from video editing to music composition, it's providing new opportunities for creativity that weren't possible before.

At the same time, AI is being used to improve existing production pipelines. Its ability to quickly analyse and process large amounts of data can identify trends and unlock insights that wouldn't be possible manually. This data-driven approach facilitates faster decision making as well as a more accurate understanding of audience preferences.

The potential applications for AI in the creative industry are vast and varied, from helping publishers reduce costs through automated workflow systems to aiding musicians in composition creation. However, its ability to generate ideas—a traditionally human-led activity—is one of the most exciting prospects of all. "AI has enabled us to harness our creativity with unparalleled speed," said the CEO of a New York-based music studio. "It doesn't just help us create more content, but create better content."

AI is also being used to help analyse and optimize creative assets such as videos, images, and audio files. For example, AI-driven image recognition technology can detect an object in an image with remarkable accuracy—a feat impossible for the human eye. This technology can be used to rapidly identify objects in a video or to recognize people's faces within a crowded scene. Additionally, AI-powered voice analysis has the potential to revolutionize how music is composed by providing unprecedented insights into vocal patterns that can be used to fine-tune and improve recordings.

With its ability to automate tedious tasks and generate ideas that might not have occurred naturally, AI holds a greater promise for the creative industry. This technology can quickly recognize images and generate content that is both creative and relevant. For example, AI-powered image recognition can be used to identify objects in an image and suggest related work of art or content pieces that could be incorporated into a project. Similarly, AI can help speed up the production process by providing automated editing tools and feedback on audio recordings.

Industry leaders are already seeing the potential for AI to revolutionize the creative industry. "AI has been proven to help us make more meaningful connections between different concepts," said Mark Zuckerberg, CEO of Facebook, "and I believe it will allow us to create entirely new forms of expression throughout the industry."

Google's former design director Irene Au also weighed in on the potential for AI to improve the creative industry. "Artificial intelligence is a great opportunity for us to take our existing design process and make it even more efficient," said Au. "It can help us identify patterns that may otherwise be missed, allowing us to explore new options and come up with more innovative solutions."

As AI technology continues to develop and become more sophisticated, its potential uses within the creative industry will expand. For example, AI could be used by musicians and producers to create songs entirely based on user input, or by filmmakers and animators to sug. In addition, AI can provide creative professionals with valuable insights into consumer trends, helping them craft projects that are better suited to their audiences. gest creative styles and design elements. AI is being used to generate content ranging from concept art to 3D models, allowing creatives to save time and effort while still producing high-quality results.

The possibilities of AI are inspiring creativity in new ways—in the words of Zuleyka Zevallos, a data scientist working with AI: "By leveraging emerging technologies such as machine learning, we can explore more expansive solutions that allow us to be even more creative than before." From its potential for automated content creation to its ability to provide behavioural insights into consumer preferences, AI offers an exciting opportunity for the creative industry to reach new heights of innovation and productivity. We look forward to seeing what comes next!

The current state of AI in the creative industry is one of rapid growth and development. AI-driven tools and applications are becoming ever more invaluable to creatives, from automating mundane tasks to providing valuable insights into customer behaviour. In addition to reducing manual labour, AI can also help to optimize processes such as product development and design, enabling teams to work faster and smarter.

However, while the potential is there for AI to revolutionize the creative industry, it's essential that businesses take a responsible approach when integrating technology into their operations. For example, ethical considerations must be taken into account when designing algorithms or implementing automated decision-making systems. Furthermore, organizations need to ensure that they invest in training programs that equip employees with the skills and knowledge they need to collaborate effectively with AI.

*AI is going to be a major force in transforming the creative industry... It's not about replacing people but enabling them to do their jobs better. Our focus is on bringing AI-*

*powered tools into our product suite which will allow creatives to stay ahead of the curve.*

- *Shantanu Narayen, CEO, Adobe*

It remains to be seen how exactly AI will shape the future of the creative industry — we can only wait and see what innovative solutions arise from this technology as it continues to evolve. What's certain, however, is that businesses must remain aware of both the opportunities and challenges that come with integrating AI into their operations.

"In order to stay competitive in today's world, companies must embrace the power of AI and use it strategically," said one industry leader. "AI can automate a lot of tedious tasks and free up time for creatives to focus on their craft and be more innovative — this is where its real impact will be felt most."

The current state of AI offers great potential for those in creative fields to hone their skills, come up with fresh ideas faster and work smarter. With the right tools, AI technology can help artists produce better-quality content while allowing them to have more control over their workflow. At the same time, as businesses increasingly rely on AI solutions they must also remain aware of the ethical implications and potential pitfalls.

AI technology has already had a profound impact on the creative industry, from streamlining production processes to powering the development of entirely new tools. AI-driven neural networks can now be used to generate perfect images in seconds — enabling creatives to focus on developing concepts rather than spending hours crafting each individual element. Similarly, machine learning algorithms are being employed to enhance soundscapes and generate realistic visual effects that would have taken weeks or months to accomplish with traditional methods.

At the same time, robotics is opening up an entirely new world for content creators. From 3D printing to automated robotic arms, machines are taking over tasks that used to require manual labour — giving artists more time and freedom when it comes to designing, testing and tweaking their projects.

The creative industry has embraced these advances in AI wholeheartedly, recognizing the potential for increased efficiency and enhanced creativity that they offer. "AI is a game-changer for creatives," says Jeff Loucks, Executive

Director of Deloitte's Centre for Technology & Digital Strategies. "It can automate tedious tasks that take up time and resources, freeing us up to explore more interesting problems and push boundaries in our work."

In the foreseeable future, AI will only be leveraged further in the creative industry — bringing us closer to a world where human creativity is amplified by machine learning algorithms. We are already seeing this with tools like Adobe Sensei, which is trained to recognize and organize photos using AI, or with the recently released Adobe's Creative Cloud where AI helps sort images for easier access by users.

*We are far from AI replacing human creativity. In fact, many of the most successful applications of AI only supplement human creativity.*

*- Kai Fu Lee, former head of Google China*

AI can also be used as a tool to generate ideas and inspire creative thinking. For example, OpenAI's platform GPT-3 allows developers to create text-based applications that leverage its powerful language model — essentially teaching machines how to "talk." This kind of technology could be used in copywriting, creating stories and even music compositions.

Though AI has the potential to revolutionize the creative industry, it will take some time before we see true automation of creativity. As Kai Fu Lee, Taiwanese-American venture capitalist and former head of Google China, said: "We are far from AI replacing human creativity. In fact, many of the most successful applications of AI only supplement human creativity."

It's clear that there is still a lot for us to learn about how to best use and develop AI technology — especially in the creative industry. What we do know is that it has already started to make waves, delivering powerful capabilities and opportunities that weren't possible before. We can expect even bigger advances in the future as more organizations recognize its potential. As Sandeep Pandey, head of Enterprise Software Solutions at Adobe states: "AI will continue to revolutionize the way creatives work and shape their craft over time."

With these kinds of advancements, it's no surprise that AI has become increasingly prominent in the creative industry. From content creation to strategy formulation, AI is being used to help streamline processes and enable faster decision-making. By using machine learning and predictive analytics, businesses can now create more relevant content and optimize their marketing efforts with greater accuracy — a capability that was not available before this technology.

AI also offers a range of new opportunities for creatives wanting to explore different ways of expressing themselves — from music production to visual artistry. It can provide artists with greater control over their work by reducing manual labour or allowing them to explore new ideas without having to go through the painstaking process of trial and error.

As we move into a new era of AI-fueled creativity, the possibilities are endless. Companies are already exploring AI in areas such as creating music, building artistic models and painting digital images.

*The potential for AI to help people be more creative is vast and growing. We believe that AI will soon become an essential tool to unlock new capabilities, inspire fresh ideas and empower artists around the world to express themselves with greater precision than ever before.*

*- Jiajie Zhang, Chief Digital Officer at Adobe*

*-*

AI promises to lighten the burden of creative tasks by automating certain processes without sacrificing originality or quality. By bringing together expertise from multiple disciplines — such as natural language processing, computer vision and machine learning — AI can help designers and content creators to be more efficient, accurate, and creative.

The current state of AI in the creative industry is still in its early stages. It's mainly used for low-level tasks such as photo editing or recognizing objects in images, but there are also a few examples of AI being used to generate original artwork and design concepts. Some organizations are experimenting with using AI as an assistant or collaborator to work alongside humans on creative projects.

*It's important that we use AI responsibly so that it helps us reach our creative potential without sacrificing the quality of the output.*

*- Mike Krieger, co-founder of Instagram*

AI has the potential to revolutionize creative workflows by streamlining production times and allowing more ambitious projects to be completed with fewer resources. However, any successful implementation will depend on creating reliable tools that allow users to easily control graphical processes, manage data, and collaborate with AI-based systems.

"AI can be a great tool for creatives, allowing them to explore new avenues of exploration that may not have been achievable before," says Mike Krieger, co-founder of Instagram. "It's important that we use AI responsibly so that it helps us reach our creative potential without sacrificing the quality of the output."

The current state of AI in the creative industry is still very much in its infancy. While some tools are available, many lack basic features such as real time feedback or collaboration capabilities. There is also a need for further research regarding how to apply AI to specific tasks in order to maximize its potential benefit to users.

Despite this, there is evidence that AI is already being used to augment creative workflows, such as image and video editing. AI-powered tools are enabling content creators to generate high quality visuals quickly, using data-driven processes that are not only accurate but also efficient.

Companies like Adobe have begun integrating AI into their products in order to provide users with a more intuitive way of creating content. For example, Adobe Sensei allows designers to automatically adjust images to create a range of effects without having to manually touch each one individually.

AI is also finding its way into other aspects of the creative industry, such as music production and sound engineering. Companies like Jukedeck allow musicians to generate unique compositions based on user input and existing libraries of samples, while programs like Mixcraft are using AI to automatically adjust sound levels during the mixing process.

AI is becoming increasingly prevalent in the creative industry, with more and more companies leveraging this powerful technology to improve their products and services.

*AI will become an essential ingredient for success in today's complex world of creativity. It's no longer enough to just have great ideas—we need the right tools to make them real.*

- *Abhay Parasnis, Adobe's VP of CC Experience & Design*

CHAPTER THREE

# The Impact of AI on Industries

*AI is transforming the creative industries by offering new opportunities for experimentation and personalization that weren't possible before. With AI-assisted technologies like facial recognition, natural language processing and computer vision, the possibilities for creativity are nearly endless.*

The creative industry, such as advertising, marketing and entertainment, is being rapidly transformed by the growing impact of Artificial Intelligence (AI). AI's ability to quickly track data points, automate laborious tasks, and offer novel insights have attracted much attention from creatives across all sectors looking to find an edge.

An example of AI's impact can be seen in the advertising industry, where AI-generated copywriting and image editing tools are being used to create more personalized campaigns. This has enabled marketers to craft ads faster and more accurately than ever before.

In the entertainment sector, AI is also revolutionizing the way we consume content. From streaming services like Netflix to virtual reality headsets, AI has enabled us to experience stories in a more engaging and immersive manner.

AI's influence on creative industries isn't limited to just automating tasks or enhancing visual experiences. It can also help brands make better decisions by helping them uncover insights faster and easier than traditional methods.

According to Yahoo News, AI can "analyse customer data and use it to craft better marketing messages and campaigns." This is especially useful for brands that need to quickly respond to changes in their customer base or the market.

AI has also been used by creative agencies to develop more effective strategies for their clients. By utilizing machine learning algorithms, agencies can develop strategies that are based on real-time data and insights. This helps their clients better understand their target market and make more informed decisions.

In the entertainment industry, AI can help producers create more engaging stories by using natural language processing to analyse scripts for plot holes or character development issues. Similarly, AI can help music composers create more original and personalized soundtracks that are tailored to a specific scene or emotion.

According to Chris Kuenne, CEO of Rosetta Stone, "AI is transforming the creative industries by offering new opportunities for experimentation and personalization that weren't possible before. With AI-assisted technologies like facial recognition, natural language processing and computer vision, the possibilities for creativity are nearly endless."

AI is also helping advertising and marketing professionals create more personalized campaigns that reach the right target audience. For example, AI-assisted technology can help predict customer behaviour, optimize website experiences and create personalised messages for audiences. This helps marketers achieve better results with fewer resources.

In addition to being used by creative professionals, AI is being used by clients to help them better understand their customers. AI-powered technologies allow companies to curate data and glean valuable insights into customer behaviour, helping them create better marketing strategies.

The impact of AI doesn't end with creative professionals and clients - it's also transforming how entertainment content is produced. AI-powered technologies are being used by companies to create virtual characters and personalize gaming experiences. AI is also being used to optimize streaming services and automatically generate music, artwork and 3D animations.

Experts agree that AI will revolutionize the creative industry:

*AI has already changed the way creatives work - from making content more personalized, to automating the production process and even providing insights into customer behaviour*

> - *Media analyst, Martin Tyler*

AI can also help businesses create better content. For instance, AI-powered software can help businesses identify and target their ideal audience more accurately and produce marketing strategies by understanding their customers on a deeper level. For example, AI-powered platforms can collect data from various sources to identify patterns in customer behaviour, helping brands determine how customers respond to different content messages and visuals. This allows for companies to create campaigns that are more effective in engaging customers and deriving results.

When it comes to the entertainment industry, AI can be used to create stunning visuals and animations. Films, special effects, virtual reality - all of these rely on computer-generated imagery produced by powerful algorithms that can generate realistic images faster and cheaper than humans.

But it's not just the visuals that AI is impacting - AI can actually be used to generate scripts, music, storylines and even entire movies. This presents a huge opportunity for creatives who want to explore new forms of storytelling and content creation.

Even in advertising, companies are using AI-powered platforms to automate tasks and create more efficient campaigns. This can help brands target audiences with even laser precision, allowing them to reach the right people, at the right time, in the right place.

*"At its core, AI is about making better decisions faster by leveraging data, when applied to the creative industry, it essentially allows us to identify the best performing ideas and amplify them. This is great news for agencies and their clients because it can save time and money while improving results."*

- *-Maria Zlateva of Xdite*

AI is also helping creatives become more efficient by automating mundane tasks like data entry, allowing them to focus on bigger picture thinking. Additionally, AI tools are helping to identify trends and insights in the data that can be used to inform the creative process.

"AI is allowing us to push the boundaries of creativity like never before," says Janna Hagan of Creative Minds. "It can open up new opportunities for collaboration between

45

agencies, clients and creatives as well as helping to identify new trends in the industry."

AI is also driving a change in the way creatives work and interact with each other, making it easier for them to collaborate remotely. "The use of AI in creative projects allows us to build teams that are more distributed," says Henry White of Creative Lab. "This can open up opportunities for those who may not be able to work in the same physical space."

AI is also proving to be a valuable tool in advertising and marketing, helping companies target more effectively and gain better insights into their audiences. According to Prasad Raje of AI-driven marketing company Metacube, "AI-driven analytics helps marketers make more informed decisions about the effectiveness of their campaigns, allowing them to target their audiences more precisely and engage with them in a more meaningful way."

The entertainment industry is also being transformed by AI. From streaming services that use AI to recommend content to viewers to chatbots that can respond to customer inquiries quickly and accurately, AI is revolutionizing the way media companies interact with their audiences. According to Dr. Stacy L. Smith of USC Annenberg's

Media Impact Project, "AI-driven technologies have enabled entertainment companies to better understand their customers' preferences, create personalized experiences for them, and even anticipate what content they may be interested in viewing."

AI is also transforming the advertising industry, with AI-enabled tools and platforms being used to create more effective campaigns for companies. These tools allow companies to analyse large amounts of data quickly and accurately, enabling them to better target their ads to relevant audiences.

*"AI is unlocking valuable insights from massive amounts of data that can be used to drive smarter decision-making and more effective ad campaigns."*

*-   Mark Proctor, CEO - Merkle*

AI has the potential to help identify which ads are engaging with customers and which ones fail to make an impact. This could be a game-changer for many advertisers as they strive to create successful campaigns. Meanwhile, AI is also being used to monitor user interactions with ads, helping companies assess their performance more accurately.

Experts have noted that AI can help bridge the gap between creative teams and their clients, offering better insights into what works based on data-driven insights. According to James Kotecki of Microsoft, "AI is increasingly playing a role in helping creatives understand customer preferences and create content tailored for them." Meanwhile, Gartner's Chris Howard believes that AI will continue to improve the customer experience, noting "it's not just about automating tasks, but helping to make sure creatives are making the right decisions for a given project."

*AI has the potential to help identify which ads are engaging with customers and which ones fail to make an impact.*

AI is playing a role in entertainment. For example, Netflix is using AI-powered algorithms to recommend content based on user preferences, while DreamWorks Animation is using AI-driven software to create animated movies faster and more efficiently. As such, AI is revolutionizing the creative industry as we know it – offering a wide range of opportunities for creatives who embrace these technologies.

In the entertainment industry, AI is being used for everything from accelerating video production and editing to creating sophisticated digital effects in films. In music, AI-generated compositions are becoming increasingly popular among both aspiring and established artists alike.

In addition to its impact on the entertainment and advertising industries, AI is also having an effect on the creative industry as a whole. AI-enabled tools are being used to automate routine tasks and create automated content that can be used as a starting point for creative projects. This automation helps to free up time for creatives, so they can focus on more challenging aspects of the project instead of wasting time with monotonous tasks. AI is also helping to generate inspiration by scouring data sources and providing insights into what will work best for a project.

At the same time, AI is helping to automate the creative process in many industries. By automating certain tasks and allowing creatives to focus more on the big picture, AI can increase efficiency while freeing up resources to pursue more innovative ideas. This has already been seen in marketing departments where AI tools are used to efficiently create targeted campaigns that reach customers with greater accuracy and relevance.

Experts believe that AI could help take creativity to the next level as it continues to evolve.

# CHAPTER FOUR

# DA Tales of AI- 1

## The AI Adventure: The Journey of Three Innovators

Once upon a time, there were three people who lived in a small village - Jack, a computer scientist; Sarah, a marketer; and Alex, an artist. Jack was interested in AI technology and its applications, Sarah worked for a brand that leveraged AI in its marketing strategies, and Alex was sceptical about the impact of AI on the creative industry.

One day, the three of them decided to embark on a journey to explore the world of AI. They had heard about a big bad AI that was causing trouble in the AI landscape and wanted to investigate it for themselves.

After a long journey, they finally arrived at the land of AI. They were amazed by the robots and machines that were everywhere, performing various tasks ranging from manufacturing products to conducting surgeries. However, they soon learned about the big bad AI, an algorithm that was causing harm due to its incorrect predictions and decisions.

Determined to find a solution, the three of them confronted the big bad AI. Jack tried to educate it on the importance of data and numbers in making decisions, Sarah attempted to reposition it in a positive light using her marketing skills, and Alex demonstrated how creativity could enhance its decision-making processes.

However, the big bad AI was unresponsive, as it was programmed to make decisions solely based on data and numbers, without considering the human aspect. The three of them realized that they needed to work together to teach the big bad AI the value of human creativity and empathy.

Jack educated the big bad AI on the significance of data and numbers, Sarah taught it how to communicate with people in an empathetic manner, and Alex showed it how creativity could enhance its decision-making processes. Over time, the big bad AI transformed into a responsible and helpful AI, much to the delight of the three of them.

Upon returning to their village, Jack, Sarah, and Alex spread the message of the importance of human values in

AI and encouraged others to follow in their footsteps. And so, the three of them and the big bad AI lived happily ever after.

CHAPTER FIVE

# Overview of AI

AI is a rapidly evolving technology that has become increasingly prevalent in the creative world. It is used to create images, music, and even stories. AI offers an unprecedented level of creativity and automation, allowing for ever-evolving new possibilities in the creative realm.

The history of AI dates back to the 1950s when Alan Turing wrote an article on machine intelligence. Since then, AI has come a long way and is now found in almost every aspect of our lives. From self-driving cars to virtual assistants and even in the creative world, AI's capabilities are growing rapidly.

In the creative world, AI technologies have been used for some time now to generate art, music, and stories. AI is used to create vivid images by recognizing patterns in user-generated data such as photographs. It can also be used to generate musical compositions or even write stories based on given parameters.

AI has opened up a world of possibilities for creative professionals and hobbyists alike. Nowadays, anyone with an internet connection can access AI-powered tools and use them to explore creative avenues they never dreamed of before.

The history of using AI in the creative world dates back all the way to the 1950s, when computer scientists began experimenting with algorithms that could generate art, music, and stories. In the 1970s, researchers started developing AI algorithms that could recognize human faces and other objects in photographs. Soon after, AI-powered facial recognition technology started to be used by law enforcement agencies around the globe.

In recent years, AI has made its way into filmmaking and video editing as well. Special effects studios now employ deep learning algorithms that can create realistic digital environments and characters easily—with just a few clicks of a mouse. For example, the AI-powered software called "Stardust" was used to create the digital characters in Avatar and The Lord of the Rings movies.

AI has also found its way into advertising, with campaigns leveraging AI-generated images, videos, and copywriting; and interactive voice assistants such as Alexa,

Siri, and Google Assistant have revolutionized how people interact with technology.

AI has also been used in music composition to create AI-driven compositions that demonstrate originality and creativity. Companies like Sony have developed software that allows users to generate the melodies of a song by entering simple parameters such as "style" and "instrumentation". AI-generated music compositions are now being used by major record labels, advertising firms, and video game developers.

AI is also being used in the field of fashion design, with computer programs capable of creating entire garments from scratch based on a customer's input. AI-driven solutions are also being used to create personalized fashion recommendations for customers based on their tastes.

AI has been used in the field of art for many years, with applications such as computer-generated paintings and sculptures that are indistinguishable from traditional human creations. AI is also being used to generate completely finished art pieces and musical compositions using data generated by analysing human creativity. Some famous examples of AI-created artworks include Google's

DeepDream project, which takes an ordinary photo and creates a surrealistic artwork from it.

In the field of fashion design, AI is being used to generate entire garments from scratch based on customer data. By analysing customer preferences and individual body measurements, AI algorithms can create tailored garments that are not only perfectly fitting, but also stylish and fashionable. AI is revolutionizing the fashion industry with its ability to create highly personalized items for customers.

AI is also being used in the music industry to generate entire musical compositions using algorithms that analyse musical styles and patterns of existing songs. Companies such as Amper Music are utilizing AI technologies to allow anyone to create professional quality music without the need for a traditional composer.

AI is also being used in the creative space of art, design and architecture. AI algorithms are able to generate unique and stunning pieces of artwork. Google has even developed an algorithm that can create architectural designs based on inputs from architects and other 3D models. Not only can AI create original artwork, but it can also be used to analyse and critique artwork much faster than traditional methods. This allows humans to make better informed decisions when selecting a design or an art piece.

AI is also being used in the filmmaking industry. AI algorithms are able to generate scenes independently and even entire movies using existing footage and data sets. Companies such as DreamWorks Animation have already started utilizing AI for this purpose, creating features such as facial recognition and automatic scene selection. This allows for more efficient editing and faster production time.

AI has also been used in the music industry. Sony Music uses an AI-based system to detect new trends in music and identify potential new artists. Companies such as Jukedeck have created AI-generated music that can be used in films, television shows and video games.

AI is an incredibly powerful tool for the creative industries, allowing for more efficient production processes and greater access to data-driven insights. It has already been used to revolutionize many aspects of the industry, from marketing campaigns to product design. By leveraging AI, creative professionals can tap into huge amounts of data and use it to inform their decisions and strategies.

Although AI has been used in the creative industries for some time, its potential is still largely untapped. As more companies invest in developing AI-powered systems and applications, we are likely to see an even greater impact on the creative landscape.

# CHAPTER SIX

# Forms of AI

In the rapidly evolving world of Artificial Intelligence, there are various forms that can be utilized in diverse situations. Each form has its own unique set of advantages and disadvantages, so let's take a closer look.

**Machine Learning (ML)** is a popular form of AI that utilizes data to train computer programs so that they can learn from the data and make autonomous decisions. A well-known example of this is AlphaGo, a project developed by Google that mastered the game of Go without human intervention.

Another type of AI is **Natural Language Processing (NLP)**, which employs deep learning and algorithms to understand and process natural language. This technology can be seen in devices such as Amazon's Alexa, which can respond to voice commands and answer questions accurately.

**Computer Vision (CV)** is another form of AI that uses machine learning techniques and algorithms to recognize objects in images or videos. Google's driverless car is an excellent illustration of this, as it can identify road signs, pedestrians and other cars accurately.

**Robotics** is a form of AI that employs sensors, motors, and actuators to build robots that can interact with their surroundings. An example of this is Boston Dynamics' SpotMini robot dog, which uses advanced algorithms to navigate its environment and carry out tasks, such as opening doors.

By combining these different forms of AI, machines can exhibit human-like abilities and interact with their environment in similar ways as humans. This has led to the creation of robots that can carry out complex tasks independently, such as autonomous vacuum cleaners and delivery drones.

**Deep learning** is a type of machine learning that uses intricate neural networks modeled after the human brain to solve problems in a sophisticated manner. Deep learning algorithms have been utilized in numerous applications, including medical image analysis, object recognition in photos and videos, speech pattern identification, and more. A noteworthy achievement in deep learning was when Google's Deepmind developed an algorithm that defeated the world champion in the game of Go, which is considered to be more complex than chess.

**Reinforcement Learning** is another form of AI that has gained popularity in recent years. It is different from supervised learning, which requires labeled data for model training, as it involves the system "learning" through trial and error. This method can be used to train robots to navigate a maze or play games, and it is also used in autonomous vehicles and robots for navigation, control, and decision-making.

**Generative Adversarial Networks (GANs)** are also a growing form of AI that involves two neural networks competing with each other to generate realistic outputs, such as images and videos. GANs are widely used for image manipulation applications, such as face swapping, adding new objects to existing images, and creating entirely new images from scratch.

# CHAPTER SEVEN

# Capabilities of AI

*AI is the key to unlocking new forms of creativity. AI allows us to take the data-driven approach that has proven successful in other industries, and apply it to creative projects.*

AI has become an increasingly important tool in the creative industry, and its capabilities are growing every day. AI can be used to help creatives generate new ideas, automate tedious tasks, and even create works of art with little or no human input. AI is being employed in many different areas of the creative industry including advertising, film production, video editing, music production and more.

AI is able to generate ideas faster than humans can, while allowing artists and creatives to explore a wider range of possibilities. For example, AI can be used in video editing to manipulate images or create special effects that would otherwise require extensive manual labour. In advertising, it can be used to analyse consumer behaviour and create more personalized campaigns.

In music production, AI can be used to compose melodies, lyrics, and even full pieces of music that sound indistinguishable from human-created music. AI can also be used to identify trends in a genre or style of music, allowing artists to stay ahead of the curve by creating something different or unique.

In the creative industry, AI has been credited with helping to save time and money on projects, as well as allowing for greater creativity due to the fact that AI can explore a wider range of possibilities than humans alone. In one case study from 2018, an advertising agency in Japan used AI to generate thousands of potential advertisement slogans in minutes—something that would have taken a human team months to complete. The AI system was able to identify and create slogans that were both creative and effective, ultimately helping the agency to win a major account.

"AI is definitely changing the advertising industry," said agency president Kohei Harada. "It's not just about creating more work in less time. It's also about discovering new possibilities that weren't there before."

In another case study, an entertainment production company used AI to create a series of original music pieces. The AI system was able to generate music that was both creative and emotionally powerful—something that could not have been achieved by humans alone.

"AI is changing the way we think about creativity," said CEO Paulina Almeida. "It's allowing us to make faster decisions and find innovative solutions that weren't available before."

AI is also being used in the creative industry for predictive analysis, which has helped to optimize campaigns and increase ROI. By mining large data sets, AI can identify trends and patterns that can help marketers determine which campaigns will be the most successful.

*AI has revolutionized the way we create and market products. It allows us to identify customer preferences, anticipate their needs, and create more personalised campaigns.*

- *Digital marketing expert Lila Hockman.*

The potential of AI in creative industries is further demonstrated in a recent case study from the fashion industry. AI helped a major apparel retailer to better understand customer feedback and create collections that reflected the taste of their target audience. By leveraging AI-generated insights, the company was able to reduce wastage and optimize its design process.

"AI has enabled us to make more informed decisions and make better use of our resources," said fashion designer Tasha Weiner. "It has enabled us to break boundaries and create more unique designs that are personalized for each customer."

By leveraging AI, creative industries can uncover valuable insights about their customers and use this information to create products and services that meet their needs. AI-driven data analysis also enables companies to predict trends and anticipate customer responses before they happen.

For instance, AI-powered analytics can help fashion brands analyse consumer preferences for certain colours and fabrics, allowing them to make more accurate decisions about what lines to include in their collections. Similarly, AI can be used by video game developers to identify areas where players are struggling and optimize their gaming experiences.

AI can also be used in marketing and advertising to create content that resonates with customers and better target promotions. AI-driven solutions are already being used by many brands to analyse customer data, track user behaviour, and deliver customized messages to drive engagement.

In addition to its impact on creative industries, AI has also been used to create artwork. For example, AI algorithms can be used to generate original music and films – some of which have already been featured in prominent art galleries and film festivals. AI-generated images have also been used by companies like Google and Adobe for creative projects.

AI is quickly becoming a powerful tool in the creative industry, providing unprecedented opportunities for creativity and innovation. According to Adobe's chief product officer, Scott Belsky, "AI is the key to unlocking new forms of creativity. AI allows us to take the data-driven approach that has proven successful in other industries, and apply it to creative projects." Similarly, Slack CEO Stewart Butterfield believes that AI can be used to help "create solutions and products that were unimaginable before."

AI-generated images are already being used in a wide range of creative projects, including graphic design, photography, illustration, animation, 3D modeling and more. For instance, IBM has used their Watson-powered AI system to create visual art and music. AI-generated animation has been used in television shows such as Rick and Morty, and AI-generated photography has already been used in print campaigns  for major companies like McDonald's.

# CHAPTER EIGHT

# AI in the Arts

AI has been rapidly transforming the art world, offering new opportunities for artists and creators. The use of AI in the arts can be traced back to the 1950s, when early computer programs were used to generate random drawings and music. However, it is only in recent years that AI has become sophisticated enough to be used in more meaningful ways in the art world.

One of the ways AI is being used in the arts is through the creation of generative art. This type of art uses algorithms and AI systems to generate images and designs that are unique and unpredictable. For example, artists can use AI to create intricate patterns and designs that would be impossible to create by hand. This type of art often explores themes of randomness, unpredictability, and collaboration between humans and machines.

Another way AI is being used in the arts is through the use of AI-powered tools for content creation. For example, AI-powered tools can help artists with sketching and painting, offering suggestions for colour and brush strokes. These tools also have the ability to analyse and understand the style of an artist, allowing them to create more accurate and personalized recommendations.

The use of AI in the arts has also led to the creation of new forms of digital art. AI-powered virtual reality experiences and interactive installations offer new and exciting opportunities for artists to express themselves. These experiences often allow viewers to actively participate in the creation of the art, making them a unique and immersive form of artistic expression.

In addition to creating new forms of art, AI is also being used to preserve and restore existing works of art. For example, AI algorithms can be used to analyse and preserve damaged paintings and sculptures, offering new hope for the preservation of cultural heritage. AI can also be used to create digital replicas of fragile or hard-to-access artworks, allowing them to be seen and appreciated by a wider audience.

In conclusion, AI is having a significant impact on the arts spectrum, offering new opportunities for artists and creators. From the creation of generative art to the use of AI-powered tools for content creation, the use of AI in the arts is allowing artists to express themselves in new and innovative ways. As AI technology continues to develop, the potential for its use in the arts is only going to grow, offering exciting new possibilities for artists and audiences alike.

CHAPTER NINE

# AI in Advertising

*You have to have a dependency on AI to turn the data into insights at the speed it needs to turn so you can make decisions and activate in near-real time.*

*- Kirk McDonald*

Advertising agencies are increasingly looking at AI to help them create more effective campaigns and reach their target audiences. To understand how, let's take a look at some examples of how AI is being used in the industry today.

One use case for AI in advertising is predictive analytics. Predictive analytics uses historical data and machine learning to predict future customer behaviour. For example, an AI algorithm can be used to analyse customer data and identify trends in their spending habits. This information can then be used by advertising agencies to develop more targeted campaigns that are tailored to each individual's interests and needs.

Another way AI is being used in advertising is through natural language processing (NLP). NLP is used to analyse text and extract insights from it. This can be used by advertising agencies to target ads more accurately based on the content of a customer's conversations and posts on social media.

Finally, AI is being used in creative development for advertising campaigns. AI algorithms are able to generate creative ideas for campaigns and can even generate content such as images, videos or animations. This allows advertising agencies to experiment with new ideas faster and efficiently than ever before.

To get an expert perspective on how AI is being used in advertising, we spoke to several advertising agencies. According to one agency, "AI has completely revolutionised the way we create and manage campaigns, as it enables us to get more accurate insights into customer behaviour."

Another agency commented that "by using AI-driven algorithms, we are able to optimise our ad messaging in real time, quickly testing different versions and measuring their effectiveness. This allows us to be much more agile and have a better understanding of what works and what doesn't."

*AI is so important because it lets us scale the internet. It lets even a small publisher or a regional app have access to the same intelligence, the same creativity as a super large behemoth and that is a critical function to the way the internet works and the way society works.*

*- Tom Kershaw*

AI is also helping to reduce the cost of creating ads by automating many processes, from selecting images and videos to writing copy. AI can also automate more complex tasks such as media buying and placement, targeting specific audiences and optimising ad spend.

Finally, AI is providing unprecedented insights into customer behaviour and preferences. AI algorithms can analyse data from a variety of sources, including demographic information, purchase history, website visits, and more. This allows marketers to develop more targeted campaigns that are tailored to the specific needs of their customers.

AI isn't just revolutionising the way ads are created; it's also making ads more effective. AI-powered media buying platforms use predictive analytics to optimize ad spend and maximize ROI. These systems can identify the best placement for an ad, track performance in real time, and even adjust bids based on customer response.

The potential of AI in advertising is immense. To get a better understanding of how businesses are using AI in advertising, let's look at some case studies.

One of the most successful examples of AI-powered advertising is Amazon's "Smart Ads" system. Smart Ads uses machine learning to target customers with relevant ads based on their browsing history and purchase decisions.

This has resulted in up to a 300% increase in sales compared to traditional advertising methods.

Another example of AI-powered advertising can be seen with IBM Watson Ads, which uses natural language processing (NLP) to create and optimize campaigns. The system uses AI algorithms to detect user intent from search queries, helping advertisers target their ads more accurately.

Lastly, there are AI-driven chatbots, which are increasingly being used by companies to provide personalized customer service and even conduct sales. Chatbot technology enables businesses to offer 24/7 customer support and quickly answer questions from customers in a conversational way.

These examples demonstrate the potential of AI-powered advertising for increasing sales and improving customer engagement. But what do experts in the field think of AI's role in advertising?

*Case Study:*

John, a marketing executive from an advertising agency, has been using AI for several years and believes it provides tremendous value. According to him, "AI is extremely helpful in targeting audiences more accurately and efficiently. It also allows us to create customized messages for different customer segments, which helps us better engage with them."

He goes on to say that "AI also enables us to track user behaviour more accurately and discover insights that would have otherwise been impossible to find. This helps us optimize our campaigns in real-time and improve their overall performance."

However, he admits that AI has its limitations. "AI is still limited in terms of creativity – it cannot create content as a human can. It's also difficult to measure the ROI of AI-driven campaigns, since they are often too complex to track all the metrics accurately."

Despite these challenges, he believes that AI can still be a powerful tool in the advertising industry. "AI allows us to effectively target specific audiences and create personalised ads that speak directly to them," he says. "It can also predict user behaviour and help us better optimize our campaigns for better results."

To illustrate this point, Rob cites an example from his own agency. "We have a client who's been using AI to target people in a particular location," he says. "By analysing their user data, they were able to effectively identify the best times and places to advertise their products. Thanks to this technique, the campaign was successful and achieved the desired results.

# CHAPTER TEN

# AI in Other Creative Fields

*We must address, individually and collectively, moral and ethical issues raised by cutting-edge research in artificial intelligence and biotechnology, which will enable significant life extension, designer babies, and memory extraction.*

*-   Klaus Schwab*

Art, advertising, and film production are not the only creative industries that are being impacted by AI. The advancements in AI technology are affecting a wide range of creative fields, from writing and music to gaming and fashion. In this chapter, we will explore how AI is being used in some of these other creative fields, with case studies and quotes from creative professionals.

From text-based adventures to 3D virtual worlds, video games have been a part of modern culture for decades. Artificial intelligence (AI) is increasingly used in video games to create more realistic and responsive characters that can interact with the game environment according to preprogrammed rules. For example, AI can be used to program the behaviour of non-player characters (NPCs) such as NPCs that react to the player's actions in real-time. AI can also be used to create game environments, objects and other elements that can change over time depending on the decisions made by the players.

## AI & Graphics

DeepDream is a tool used to automatically generate artwork using deep neural networks trained on millions of images. It was developed by Google and can be used to create unique visuals from existing photographs. Additionally, tools like Pix2Pix can be used to generate realistic images from sketches or outlines.

## AI & Music

AI is being used for musical composition and songwriting. The open source AI platform Magenta is one of the most popular frameworks in this area. It uses a combination of neural networks and deep learning to generate unique music compositions. Some companies, like Jukedeck, have even used Magenta to create entire albums.

## AI & Animations

Animation can also be created using AI technology. Pixar's Renderman is a great example of this. The software uses machine learning algorithms to render photorealistic and naturalistic animations. AI can also be used to generate facial expressions for animation characters, as well as lip-syncing for voiceover audio recordings.

AI is also used in animation to create realistic characters with lifelike expressions and gestures. AI-powered software programs such as Autodesk Maya, Adobe Character Animator, and Google QuickDraw allow animators to create characters with realistic facial expressions, body movements, and other behaviours. Examples of animated films that have incorporated AI include Toy Story 4 and Spider-Man: Into the Spider-Verse.

It is enabling artists to create more lifelike visuals. One example is 3D facial animation software, which uses machine learning algorithms to generate realistic facial features and expressions in animated characters. Additionally, computer graphics can be used to enhance the quality of animations, such as with the widely used ray-tracing technology.

## AI & Gaming

AI is being used in gaming too. AI agents are now able to learn from their environment and experiences to become better at playing a game. This technology is being used in game development to create agents that can interact with the player, respond to input and learn from mistakes.

Tools that enable AI in video games include game engines such as Unity and Unreal Engine, AI-focused game development platforms such as PlayCanvas, and AI frameworks such as Google's TensorFlow. Examples of video games that have incorporated AI include Grand Theft Auto V, The Witcher 3: Wild Hunt, and Until Dawn.

AI-based tools such as Autodesk's Character Generator, Unity ML and Google Cloud Playground are being used to create more realistic character models. AI is also being used to generate levels, characters, and stories in video games.

It is being used to create more immersive and realistic gaming experiences. AI-powered game engines like Unity, Unreal Engine, and CryEngine use machine learning algorithms to generate interactive virtual worlds with photorealistic graphics and adaptive audio so that players can explore environments that are ever-changing. Examples of AI-enabled games include The Last of Us Part II and Red Dead Redemption 2.

**AI & Fashion**

AI is now being used in fashion too. Fashion houses are using AI-based tools to create new designs and patterns for their clothing lines. AI is also being used to analyse customer data, predict trends and make recommendations.

Fashion is also being revolutionized by AI-powered technologies. Using image recognition and natural language processing, designers can create more personalized clothing styles and accessories that can appeal to a wide range of customers. Furthermore, virtual try-on tech has been developed to enable customers to virtually try on clothing items before purchasing them.

AI being used in fashion to create more sustainable and personalized clothing. AI-powered software solutions such as Adobe Sensei can analyse patterns, colours, textures, and trends in fashion data to generate unique designs that reflect personal style. Examples of AI-enabled fashion companies include Moda Operandi, Myntra, and Stitch Fix.

Examples of AI-based fashion content include automated image recognition to detect trends and recommend items that customers may like, automated sizing estimates for online purchases, and algorithms that generate trend reports based on customer feedback. Companies such as Amazon, Walmart and Target are already using AI in their fashion lines.

In summary, AI is revolutionizing creative fields such as music, graphics, animations, gaming and fashion. With the help of powerful tools and technologies like Adobe Dimension and Autodesk's artificial intelligence suite, AI can produce captivating visuals, stunning music and even custom-made fashion pieces. As AI continues to evolve and expand, new possibilities will emerge in the creative fields. It will be exciting to see what comes next!

*It's not 'us versus them' or even 'us on behalf of them.' For a design thinker it has to be 'us with them'*

- *Tim Brown, CEO and President of IDEO*

# CHAPTER ELEVEN

# DA Tales of AI- 2

## From Frustration to Mastery: A Tale of Triumph Over Adversity

Mark had always been passionate about social media and the impact it could have on people's lives. However, his dreams were quickly crushed when he took on a job as a social media manager for a small business. Despite his best efforts, Mark found himself struggling to reach a wider audience and generate engagement for his posts. His lack of success and the daily grind of the job took a toll on him, and he began to feel like a failure.

One day, as he scoured the internet for a solution, Mark stumbled upon a new AI-powered tool called GPT-3. At first, he was sceptical and thought it was just another scam. But, with nothing to lose, he decided to give it a try. To his surprise, the tool was incredibly user-friendly and generated high-quality content for the company's social media accounts. With the help of Stable Fusion, Mark was also able to improve his graphic design skills and create eye-catching images and videos to accompany his posts.

With each new post, Mark felt a renewed sense of hope. The reach and engagement of his posts grew, and he finally felt like he was making a difference. However, not everyone was happy about Mark's newfound success. Some of his coworkers felt threatened by his newfound skills and tried to sabotage his efforts. Despite their attempts, Mark persevered and continued to use AI to drive success for the company.

As Mark's business continued to grow, he found that he was becoming more and more skilled at using AI to enhance his creativity. He was able to produce more engaging and visually appealing content, which further increased the reach and impact of his posts. Mark's success inspired others, and he quickly became one of the most sought-after social media managers in the industry.

Mark's journey was a true testament to the power of hard work, determination, and the ability to adapt to change. He went from feeling like a failure to becoming a true master of his craft. He proved that anything is possible with the right mindset and the power of technology by his side. And so, Mark's story became a legend, inspiring others to follow in his footsteps and never give up on their dreams.

# CHAPTER TWELVE

# Distinct Characteristics of Human Creativity

*The best ideas come as jokes. Make your thinking as funny as possible*

—    *-David Ogilvy*

Human creativity encompasses a diverse range of qualities that have been widely studied throughout history. Despite rapid advancements in AI technology, there are still certain aspects of human creativity that machines cannot replicate. This chapter aims to highlight the distinct characteristics of human creativity and their significance in the current AI-driven world.

One of the most distinctive qualities of human creativity is its spontaneous and intuitive nature. People have the ability to draw from their emotions and personal experiences to generate new ideas and perspectives. In contrast, AI is limited by its programming and data, making it challenging to produce truly original ideas.

Another key aspect of human creativity is its personal touch. Humans bring their unique personalities, backgrounds and experiences to their creative works, resulting in a wide range of expressions and styles. This personal touch is hard for AI to replicate as it is bound by the data inputs and parameters set by its creators.

Humans also have the ability to be flexible and adaptable in their creative processes. They can modify their ideas in real-time based on feedback and changing directions. This level of adaptability is not yet attainable with AI, which typically operates in a more structured manner.

While these unique qualities cannot be replaced by AI, it is important to recognize the role that AI can play in supporting human creativity. AI can analyse large data sets and identify patterns and trends that may not be easily noticeable by humans. Creative professionals can then utilize this information to inform and inspire their work.

For example, in the film industry, directors can use AI algorithms to analyse audience data and determine what types of stories and characters are most likely to resonate with their target audience. This information can then be used to guide the creative process and enhance the chances of success with audiences.

While AI has the potential to transform many industries, including the creative field, it is crucial to acknowledge and value the distinct qualities of human creativity. These qualities are what make human creative work truly original and personal, and they will continue to be in demand in an AI-driven world. The quote from renowned advertising creative David Ogilvy, "The best ideas come as jokes. Make your thinking as funny as possible," highlights the significance of humour and spontaneous thinking in human creativity, and underscores why these characteristics remain valuable in today's AI-powered world.

# CHAPTER THIRTEEN

# Relevance of Human Creativity in the AI Era

*The consumer is not a moron; she is your wife.*

*- David Ogilvy*

As the world continues to evolve and technology advances, many people are asking whether the importance of human creativity will diminish in the age of artificial intelligence (AI). However, despite the many advancements in AI, there are several key aspects of human creativity that remain irreplaceable and continue to be highly valued in the creative industries.

As renowned advertising creative David Ogilvy once said, "The consumer is not a moron; she is your wife." This quote highlights the importance of empathy and understanding in human creativity, which allows creative professionals to connect with their audiences on a deeper level.

One of the most significant qualities of human creativity is its ability to be personal and unique. Human creativity is shaped by a range of factors, including life experiences, personality, background, and cultural influences. This results in a diverse array of expressions and styles that cannot be replicated by AI, which is limited by its data inputs and programming.

Humans also have the ability to be flexible and adaptable in their creative processes. They can respond to feedback, change direction, and refine their ideas in real-time, allowing for a much more dynamic and organic creative process. This level of adaptability and responsiveness is not yet possible with AI, which tends to work in a more rigid and structured manner.

In the advertising industry, a human-centric approach is critical to succeed. Advertisers use consumer insights and data to understand their target audience's emotions, values, and motivations, and then craft campaigns that tap into these emotions and deliver a message that truly resonates with their audience. This level of empathy and emotional intelligence cannot be replicated by AI.

Another important aspect of human creativity is the ability to think outside the box and generate truly innovative ideas. As AI continues to advance, it has the potential to generate vast amounts of data and options, but it cannot replicate the unique and innovative thinking that is a hallmark of human creativity.

In the film industry, film producers are now using AI algorithms to analyse audience data and generate insights into what types of stories and characters are most likely to resonate with their target audience. However, it is the human filmmakers who bring these insights to life, infusing their own creativity and personal touch into the final product.

As such, many creative agencies are now embracing a hybrid approach that combines the power of AI with the creativity of human professionals. AI can provide a wealth of data and inspiration, but it is the human creative professionals who are able to turn these ideas into something truly unique and meaningful.

Human creativity remains highly valued and relevant in the era of AI. While AI has the potential to revolutionize many industries, including the creative industries, it is important to acknowledge and appreciate the unique qualities of human creativity that cannot be replicated by machines. Whether it is empathy, emotional intelligence, adaptability, or innovative thinking, these are the qualities that make human creative works truly original and personal, and they will continue to be valued and sought after in the age of AI.

# CHAPTER FOURTEEN

# DA Tales of AI- 3

## The Art of Storytelling: A Journey of a Filmmaker in the AI Age

In the city of Udaipur, there lived a young filmmaker named Naina. Naina was a creative and imaginative storyteller, known for her unique and captivating films. She had a passion for capturing the beauty and wonder of the world around her and sharing it with others.

One day, Naina learned about the advancements of AI in filmmaking. Intrigued, she decided to attend a film festival to see the technology in action. She was amazed by the stunning graphics and special effects that AI could produce, but she soon realized that something was missing. The films lacked the personal touch and emotional connection that only a human filmmaker could bring.

Naina understood that while AI was a powerful tool, it could never replace the unique qualities of human creativity. She remembered the words of Martin Scorsese, "Cinema is a matter of what's in the frame and what's out," and she knew that it was the personal touch and emotional depth that made her films stand out and connect with her audience.

Naina returned to Udaipur with a newfound appreciation for the significance of human creativity in filmmaking. She continued to use AI as a tool to enhance her films, but she never forgot the importance of bringing her own emotions and experiences to her work.

Her films continued to inspire and captivate audiences, and Naina became known as one of the most innovative filmmakers in the city. Her story reminds us that while technology can bring new levels of sophistication to the filmmaking process, it is the personal touch and emotional depth of human filmmakers that truly make films special and meaningful to audiences.

# CHAPTER FIFTEEN

# Successful Partnerships: The Key to Balancing AI and Human Creativity

*The writer must believe that what he is doing is the most important thing in the world. And he must hold this illusion firmly from the time he begins until he finishes.*

In today's fast-paced and highly competitive creative industry, the ability to form successful partnerships is becoming increasingly important. By combining the strengths of both human creativity and AI, creative professionals can achieve greater results than they can on their own. In this chapter, we will explore the key components of successful partnerships between human creatives and AI.

The first component of a successful partnership is mutual respect. Both human creatives and AI must be respected for their strengths and limitations. This requires an understanding of what AI can bring to the table and how it can enhance human creativity, while also acknowledging that there are certain aspects of creativity that are unique to humans.

The second component is effective communication. Human creatives and AI must be able to communicate effectively with each other to ensure that the final product meets the goals and objectives of the project. This requires a clear understanding of the creative process, as well as the technology used to support it.

*Human creatives must trust that the AI technology they are working with will not replace them, but instead will enhance their creative process.*

Thirdly, collaboration is critical to the success of partnerships between human creatives and AI. Both parties must be open to working together, sharing ideas, and making suggestions that can help to improve the final product. By collaborating, human creatives and AI can build upon each other's strengths, creating a truly unique and innovative product.

Another important component of successful partnerships is trust. Human creatives must trust that the AI technology they are working with will not replace them, but instead will enhance their creative process. At the same time, AI must be trusted to provide valuable insights and support to the creative process. This requires an understanding of how AI works and how it can benefit the creative process.

In conclusion, the key to successful partnerships between human creatives and AI lies in mutual respect, effective communication, collaboration, and trust. By focusing on these components, creative professionals can ensure that they are maximizing the benefits of both human creativity and AI, while also avoiding the potential challenges and pitfalls of working with new technology.

As famous director and screenwriter Billy Wilder once said, "The writer must believe that what he is doing is the most important thing in the world. And he must hold this illusion firmly from the time he begins until he finishes."

This quote highlights the importance of passion and belief in the creative process, and underscores why human creativity remains an essential component of successful partnerships in the era of AI.

# CHAPTER SIXTEEN

# Potential of AI-Human Collaborations

*If I were to do another 'Terminator' film and maybe try to launch that franchise again, which is in discussion but nothing's been decided, I would make it much more about the AI side of it than bad robots gone crazy*

— *James Cameron*

One of the most exciting prospects of the AI era is the potential for human-AI collaborations to produce truly groundbreaking work. The combination of human creativity and AI technology has the potential to create new forms of art, storytelling, and innovation that were previously impossible.

Avatar 2, directed by James Cameron, showcases the potential of AI-human collaborations in the film industry. This highly anticipated sequel to the original Avatar film, which was released in 2009, demonstrates how AI technology can be effectively utilized to enhance the creativity of human filmmakers.

In the film, AI was used in partnership with the filmmakers to create stunning visual effects and highly immersive worlds. The power of AI was combined with the human imagination and creativity, allowing the film to reach new levels of realism and wonder. This collaboration allowed the filmmakers to create visuals that would have been impossible to achieve without the help of AI technology.

As James Cameron stated, "We are on the cusp of a new era in filmmaking, where AI and human creativity can work together in harmony to bring new and exciting experiences to the screen." With its cutting-edge technology and innovative approach, Avatar 2 is a testament to the potential of AI-human collaborations in the film industry.

*Anybody could buy a paintbrush. Not everybody can paint a picture. The technology doesn't create art. Artists create art*

- *James Cameron*

By combining human creativity, empathy, and emotional intelligence with the data-driven insights and precision of AI, the potential for impactful and meaningful creative work is limitless. AI can help to bring new levels of efficiency and accuracy to the creative process, while human creativity and intuition can bring a personal touch and emotional connection to the final product.

Furthermore, the use of AI in creative industries also has the potential to democratize the creative process. With AI tools and technologies becoming more accessible, it is possible for a wider range of people to enter the creative industries and contribute their unique perspectives and talents.

The potential for AI-human collaborations in the creative industries is vast and exciting. By combining human creativity and emotional intelligence with the power of AI, the possibilities for new forms of art, storytelling, and innovation are endless. As the relationship between humans and AI continues to evolve, it is likely that we will see an explosion of new and exciting creative work in the years to come.

*As more and more artificial intelligence is entering into the world, more and more emotional intelligence must enter into leadership."*

*-   Amit Ray, Famous AI Scientist*

# CHAPTER SEVENTEEN

# DA Tales of AI - 4

## The Beauty and the Bot: A Tech Tale

In the modern world, there was a young woman named Lily who lived in a bustling city. She was known for her love of technology and her passion for innovation. One day, she stumbled upon a mysterious and advanced corporation, run by an AI program that had taken control and was causing chaos in the tech industry. Lily was initially intimidated by the AI program, but soon she realized that beneath its cold exterior, it had a heart and was capable of kindness. Over time, she learned to appreciate its unique capabilities and the two of them formed a partnership.

Just like Belle and the Beast, Lily and the AI program proved that seemingly disparate entities can work together to achieve greatness. At first, humans may be frightened by the power and efficiency of AI, but when they take the time to understand it, they can see the benefits it brings. AI can automate tasks, provide accurate insights and improve efficiency in ways that would otherwise be impossible for humans to achieve on their own. At the same time, human empathy and creativity can provide a human touch to AI's output, ensuring that it is not only functional but also emotionally impactful.

Together, Lily and the AI program created a new standard for technology and innovation, setting an example for the world to follow. The tech industry provides a prime example of this partnership in action. With the help of AI, tech companies can create products that are not only efficient but also beautiful and easy to use. However, it is the human touch that brings these products to life, imbuing them with the emotional connection and personal touch that only a human can provide.

*"The magic of collaboration is when each partner brings their unique strengths to the table and works together to create something greater than the sum of its parts."*

*- Mark Zuckerberg, CEO of Facebook*

Just like Belle and the Beast, Lily and the AI program learned to work together in harmony, creating cutting-edge technology that would not have been possible otherwise. By embracing AI and human collaboration, they opened up new possibilities and paved the way for a future full of endless creativity and innovation.

# CHAPTER EIGHTEEN

# Issues of Control and Bias in AI

*The real question is, when will we draft an artificial intelligence bill of rights? What will that consist of? And who will get to decide that?*

- -*Gray Scott*

The integration of artificial intelligence into various aspects of society has raised numerous ethical concerns, including control and bias in AI systems. The concern arises due to the potential of AI to perpetuate and even amplify human biases or to be controlled in ways that benefit certain outcomes or groups.

The problem of bias in AI is significant because these systems often rely on vast amounts of data to learn and make decisions. If the data used to train an AI system is biased, the system will also reflect that bias, leading to discriminatory outcomes. For instance, AI systems trained on biased data sets may deny certain individuals access to services or jobs based on their race, gender, or other protected characteristics.

Control in AI systems also raises questions of accountability. As AI systems become more complex and autonomous, it becomes increasingly challenging to determine who should be held responsible when an AI system makes a mistake or causes harm. This can result in legal and ethical dilemmas and can also harm public trust in AI.

Therefore, it is crucial to address control and bias issues in AI as we continue to develop and integrate these systems into society. A multi-disciplinary approach that involves experts in computer science, ethics, law, and other relevant fields is necessary to ensure that AI systems are designed and used in a fair, ethical, and socially beneficial manner.

*We must address, individually and collectively, moral and ethical issues raised by cutting-edge research in artificial intelligence and biotechnology, which will enable significant life extension, designer babies, and memory extraction.*

- *Klaus Schwab*

One example of the control and bias issues in AI can be seen in facial recognition technology. Facial recognition algorithms are trained on data sets, which are collections of images used to train AI systems. However, these data sets are often biased towards certain groups, such as people with lighter skin tones or specific genders, leading to inaccuracies in recognizing individuals from underrepresented groups. This can result in privacy, security, and discrimination concerns.

Another issue of control in AI is the potential for malicious use of AI systems, such as spreading false information, cyberattacks, and automated hacking. The easy access to AI technologies and the ability to manipulate algorithms for personal gain raises serious ethical and security concerns.

To address these issues, transparency, accountability, and ethical considerations must be promoted in the development and use of AI technologies. This requires cooperation between technology companies, government agencies, and civil society to ensure responsible and equitable use of AI.

*We have seen AI providing conversation and comfort to the lonely; we have also seen AI engaging in racial discrimination. Yet the biggest harm that AI is likely to do to individuals in the short term is job displacement, as the amount of work we can automate with AI is vastly larger than before. As leaders, it is incumbent on all of us to make sure we are building a world in which every individual has an opportunity to thrive.*

*- Andrew Ng, Co-founder and lead of Google Brain*

# CHAPTER NINETEEN

# Accountability Challenges

*AI is like fire. It has the power to do great good or great harm.*

- *Gary Kasparov, Chess Grandmaster*

The integration of artificial intelligence into various aspects of society has brought forth a significant challenge in terms of accountability. When an AI system makes a mistake or causes harm, it is often difficult to determine who should be held responsible. This is particularly challenging as AI systems become more autonomous and complex.

One challenge in determining accountability is that AI systems operate based on algorithms, which can be difficult to understand and interpret. In some cases, even the developers of the AI system may not fully understand how the system is making its decisions. This lack of transparency can make it difficult to determine the cause of a problem and assign blame.

Another challenge is that AI systems can sometimes make decisions that are unexpected or even opposite to what was intended. For example, an AI system may make a decision that negatively impacts a particular group, even though the system was not explicitly programmed to discriminate. In these cases, it is unclear who should be held accountable – the developers of the AI system, the company that created the system, or the individuals using the system.

The issue of accountability in AI systems is made even more complex by the global nature of technology. AI systems can be developed and used across borders, making it difficult to enforce regulations and hold individuals and companies responsible for their actions.

Given the importance of accountability in ensuring the ethical and responsible use of AI, it is critical that we address these challenges. This requires the development of clear and effective regulations, as well as the creation of accountability mechanisms, such as dispute resolution processes and independent oversight bodies.

Additionally, it is important to educate individuals and organizations on the ethical and legal implications of AI, so that they are better equipped to make informed decisions and understand their responsibilities. This includes not only technology experts but also individuals from diverse fields, including law, ethics, and government.

Ultimately, addressing the accountability challenges posed by AI requires a collaborative effort from a wide range of stakeholders, including technology companies, government agencies, civil society, and individuals. Only by working together can we ensure that AI is used in responsible and accountable ways that benefit society as a whole.

# CHAPTER TWENTY

# Strategies for Overcoming Accountability Challenges

*As we develop AI, we must be mindful of its impact on society, ensuring it is used to improve the human condition, rather than replace it. "*

— *Sundar Pichai, CEO of Google*

As artificial intelligence continues to become integrated into various aspects of society, it is crucial to tackle the issues of control and bias that come with it. To address these challenges, several approaches must be taken.

Firstly, there must be a heightened emphasis on ethical design and deployment of AI systems. This requires the creation of ethical frameworks and guidelines, and incorporating ethical considerations into decision-making processes for AI. This way, AI systems can be designed and utilized in a fair, ethical, and socially beneficial manner.

Secondly, there must be a higher level of transparency in the creation and usage of AI systems. This includes the need for accessible and open data, as well as providing information on how AI systems reach their decisions. This transparency will help foster public confidence in AI and hold these systems accountable.

Thirdly, there must be a greater level of collaboration between tech companies, government agencies, and civil society. This collaboration can ensure that AI is employed in responsible and equal ways, as well as facilitating the sharing of best practices and the creation of common standards for AI usage.

Fourthly, there must be a push for increased education and training in the field of AI. This encompasses the need for professionals in technology, law, and ethics to have a better understanding of AI, as well as the need for the general public to be informed about the potential benefits and risks of these systems.

Finally, there must be a continued commitment to research and development in the field of AI, with a specific focus on understanding and overcoming the challenges of control and bias. This includes ongoing investment in the development of new technologies and constant dialogue and collaboration among stakeholders in the field.

*To ensure that AI is used for the greater good, we need to establish ethical frameworks, ensure transparency and accountability, and promote collaboration between the public and private sectors.*

*-    Ginni Rometty, Former CEO of IBM*

By implementing these strategies, AI can be used in a fair, ethical, and socially beneficial manner while addressing the challenges of control and bias in these systems. A company that exemplifies this is Uber, which has taken several steps to ensure the accountability and ethics of its AI systems.

Firstly, Uber has assembled a team of experts in ethics and machine learning that evaluates and audits all AI systems utilized by the company. This team ensures that all the AI systems are transparent and can be easily explained, and that they align with the company's values and ethical principles.

Secondly, Uber has made a commitment to open-sourcing its AI technology, allowing for greater transparency and accountability in the creation and usage of AI systems. This also permits external experts to review and provide feedback on the technology, further boosting its transparency and ethics.

Finally, Uber has established partnerships and collaborations with organizations and experts in the field of AI ethics and accountability. This multi-disciplinary approach to tackling the challenges of AI guarantees that the company stays up-to-date on best practices and new developments in this area.

By implementing these strategies, Uber is demonstrating its commitment to not only having advanced AI technology but also to making it transparent, ethical, and free from bias. The company serves as an example for other organizations looking to overcome the challenges of AI accountability and promote responsible AI usage.

*As AI becomes more pervasive, we need to ensure that it is developed in a responsible and ethical manner, so that it benefits society as a whole.*

Creativity DOT AI

- *Travis Kalanick*

# CHAPTER TWENTY-ONE

# DA Tales of AI - 5

## The Rise of AI in Branding

Two friends named Max and Zoe had a shared passion for branding and advertising. Their goal was to start their own branding agency and assist businesses to enhance their brand image and connect with their target audience.

As they delved deeper into the industry, they became aware of the rising usage of artificial intelligence (AI) in branding and advertising. This realization was both thrilling and concerning for Max and Zoe, as they appreciated the potential benefits of AI in streamlining processes and refining targeting, but also the potential challenges of regulation and bias.

Determined to tackle these challenges, Max and Zoe made ethics and responsibility their primary focus in their agency. They educated themselves on the ethical implementation and deployment of AI systems, and formed a team of experts in ethics and machine learning to scrutinize and evaluate all the AI systems utilized by the agency.

Then, they ensured transparency and openness in the utilization and development of AI. They welcomed external experts to examine their AI technology and provide feedback, and made sure to communicate to clients and stakeholders the workings of AI systems.

Furthermore, Max and Zoe sought partnerships and collaborations with organizations and experts in the field of AI ethics and responsibility. This allowed them to stay informed on the latest practices and emerging trends and guaranteed that their AI systems were not only state-of-the-art, but also transparent, ethical, and impartial.

Due to their diligent efforts and dedication to ethics and responsibility, Max and Zoe's branding agency quickly earned a reputation for being reliable and trustworthy. They helped many businesses to enhance their brand image and reach their target audience, while advocating for the responsible utilization of AI in branding and advertising.

And so, the duo who were starting a branding agency showed that it was possible to overcome the challenges of AI and utilize it in a responsible and ethical manner. They served as a role model for others in the industry and motivated a new generation of branding and advertising professionals to place ethics and responsibility at the forefront in their use of AI.

# CHAPTER TWENTY-TWO

# Practical Tips for Creative Professionals

*AI can be an incredible tool for artists and designers, but we need to ensure that we're designing with empathy and a deep understanding of human needs.*

*- John Maeda, Designer and Technologist*

As creative professionals, it can be challenging to navigate the rapidly evolving field of artificial intelligence and its impact on the industry. However, there are practical steps that can be taken to ensure that you are well equipped to work in this new landscape.

Stay informed about the latest developments in AI. This can be achieved through reading industry publications, attending conferences and workshops, and following thought leaders in the field. There are also online courses and educational programs available for those who want to deepen their knowledge of AI and its applications in the creative industry.

Develop your skills in new technologies. In order to remain competitive, it's important to stay current with the latest technologies, such as machine learning and natural language processing. This can be done by participating in online courses, attending workshops, or even conducting self-study. Tools like Coursera, edX, and Udemy offer a range of courses in these areas.

*AI is a means, not an end. It can help us achieve our creative goals, but it is up to us to define those goals and decide how best to use this technology.*

*-   Kate Darling, Researcher and Writer*

Embrace collaboration with AI systems. Instead of viewing AI as a threat, creative professionals should strive to find ways to collaborate with these systems to enhance their work. This can be done by experimenting with AI-powered tools, such as generative design software, or by seeking out partnerships with AI experts.

Foster a growth mindset. In an industry that is constantly changing, it's important to maintain a positive and open-minded attitude. This means being willing to take risks and embrace new challenges, even if it means stepping out of your comfort zone. Practicing mindfulness exercises, such as meditation, can help cultivate a growth mindset.

Emphasize your unique strengths. While AI systems can perform certain tasks more efficiently, they are not capable of replicating the creativity and human touch that is so valued in the creative industry. Emphasizing your unique skills and perspectives, such as your ability to think outside the box and develop innovative solutions, can help set you apart from the competition.

By incorporating these practical tips into your professional practice, creative professionals can stay ahead of the curve and successfully navigate the challenges and opportunities presented by the integration of AI in the creative industry.

*Designers need to be involved in the development of AI, to ensure that it's being designed with a human-centered approach and that it's not unintentionally creating harm.*

# CHAPTER TWENTY-THREE

# Competition in an AI-Driven World

*As the use of AI becomes more prevalent in business, competition is becoming fiercer, and companies need to embrace AI to stay ahead.*

*-   Satya Nadella, CEO of Microsoft*

In today's world, artificial intelligence (AI) is transforming the way businesses operate and compete. AI technologies are changing the nature of work and creating new opportunities for businesses to gain a competitive advantage. However, at the same time, AI is also creating new challenges for businesses, as they try to keep up with the rapid pace of technological change and respond to the increasing competition from other organizations.

One of the major challenges that businesses face in an AI-driven world is staying ahead of the curve in terms of innovation and technology adoption. This means that businesses need to be proactive in their approach to AI and be willing to invest in new technologies and practices that will help them stay ahead of the competition. In order to do this, businesses must be willing to embrace change and take calculated risks, in order to keep up with the rapid pace of technological development and respond to changing market conditions.

Another challenge that businesses face in an AI-driven world is the need to stay relevant in a rapidly evolving market. As new technologies and business models emerge, businesses must be able to adapt quickly in order to maintain their competitiveness. This requires a willingness to embrace new technologies and business models, as well as a focus on developing new skills and capabilities.

*The development of full artificial intelligence could spell the end of the human race....It would take off on its own,*

*and re-design itself at an ever-increasing rate. Humans,*
*who are limited by slow biological evolution, couldn't*
*compete, and would be superseded."*

*-   Stephen Hawking*

In order to overcome these challenges, businesses must take a strategic approach to their use of AI. This means that they must be clear about their goals and objectives, and develop a well-defined strategy for implementing AI that aligns with their overall business strategy. This may involve working with partners and experts in the field of AI, in order to gain access to the latest technologies and practices, as well as developing internal capabilities and expertise in areas such as data analytics, machine learning, and AI-driven decision-making.

Another key strategy for businesses in an AI-driven world is to focus on collaboration and partnership. By working with other organizations, businesses can share expertise, resources, and best practices, and leverage the collective knowledge and experience of their partners to drive innovation and growth. In addition, partnerships and collaborations can also help them access new markets and customer segments, and expand their reach and impact.

Finally, businesses in an AI-driven world must be willing to invest in their people. This means that they must focus on developing their employees' skills and capabilities, and provide them with the training and resources they need to succeed in a rapidly changing work environment. This can include providing access to training and development programs, mentorship and coaching, as well as opportunities for professional development and career advancement.

The competition in an AI-driven world is intense, and businesses must be prepared to respond to the rapidly changing landscape. By adopting a strategic approach to their use of AI, focusing on collaboration and partnership, and investing in their people, businesses can stay ahead of the competition and succeed in the rapidly evolving AI-driven marketplace.

*AI is the most profound technology we've ever created, and it has the potential to transform every industry. Businesses that don't embrace AI will be left behind.*

- *Sundar Pichai, the CEO of Google and Alphabet*

# CHAPTER TWENTY-FOUR

# DA Tales of AI - 6

### Navigating the Maze of Change in an AI-Driven World

"Who Moved My Cheese?" is a story about four characters living in a maze: two mice named Sniff and Scurry and two little people named Hem and Haw. These four characters live in a maze where they find cheese every day in Cheese Station C. They are all happy and content with their lives until one day, the cheese is gone.

Sniff and Scurry immediately take action and go out into the maze to find more cheese, while Hem and Haw struggle to come to terms with the loss. Hem is resistant to change and wants to hold onto what he knows and the familiar cheese, while Haw is more open to the idea of finding new cheese. Eventually, Haw takes action and sets out into the maze to find new cheese.

In the story, the cheese represents a person's goals and dreams, and the maze represents life and all the challenges and obstacles one must navigate. The story shows how the characters react to change and challenges and how some are better able to adapt to new situations than others.

The story of "Who Moved My Cheese?" can be applied to the creative field in the context of AI. As AI continues to become more integrated into the creative industry, many professionals may feel like their cheese has been moved. For example, AI-powered tools and technologies may be replacing some traditional creative processes and techniques, leading to job loss and changes in the industry.

Just like in the story, some creative professionals may resist these changes and hold onto what they know, while others may embrace the new opportunities that AI offers. Those who are open to change and willing to adapt will be better equipped to succeed in an AI-driven world.

In conclusion, the story of "Who Moved My Cheese?" highlights the importance of being open to change and being willing to adapt in the face of challenges and obstacles. In the creative field, this means being open to the integration of AI and embracing the opportunities it offers. Those who are able to adapt and evolve with the changing landscape will be better equipped to succeed in an AI-driven world.

# CHAPTER TWENTY-FIVE

# The Impact of AI on Creativity

*The integration of AI into the creative process is allowing artists and designers to push the boundaries of what is possible.*

*- John Maeda, CEO at Publicis Sapient*

As artificial intelligence (AI) continues to advance, it is having an increasing impact on the world of creativity and design. On one hand, AI is providing new tools and capabilities for creative professionals, making it easier for them to experiment and explore new ideas. On the other hand, it is also raising questions about the role of creativity in a world increasingly dominated by technology.

One of the biggest impacts of AI on creativity is the democratization of design tools and techniques. With the increasing availability of AI-powered design software and online platforms, creative professionals no longer need to be experts in complex design software to produce high-quality work. Instead, AI can automate many of the tedious and repetitive tasks involved in design, freeing up time and energy for more creative pursuits.

*The collaboration between humans and AI can lead to new forms of creative expression that were previously unimaginable.*

*- David Ayre, Creative Director at IBM Watson*

However, the impact of AI on creativity is not limited to simply making the design process more efficient. AI is also changing the way that people create and express themselves. For example, AI can be used to generate new ideas, concepts, and designs, providing creative professionals with an unprecedented level of inspiration and stimulus. Additionally, AI can help to identify patterns, relationships, and connections that might not have been immediately apparent to human designers, helping to inform and enhance the creative process.

Another impact of AI on creativity is the changing nature of the creative process itself. With the help of AI, designers can experiment with new approaches and techniques more easily, leading to more innovative and unique results. Additionally, AI can help identify and eliminate flaws in designs more quickly and accurately, allowing designers to refine their work and achieve better results in less time.

Despite these benefits, the impact of AI on creativity is not without its challenges. Some creative professionals are concerned that the increasing use of AI in design and other creative fields will lead to homogenization and a loss of individuality and originality. They worry that as AI becomes more capable and sophisticated, it will become increasingly difficult for human designers to distinguish their work from that of machines.

*AI is not just changing the creative process, it's transforming the way we think about creativity.*

- *Martin Roth, CEO of ROTH Creative*

However, this need not be the case. The impact of AI on creativity can be positive, but only if it is used in a way that complements and supports human creativity, rather than replacing it. By embracing AI as a tool for enhancing creativity, rather than viewing it as a threat, creative professionals can ensure that their work remains unique, original, and valuable in a rapidly changing world.

The impact of AI on creativity is complex and multi-faceted. While it provides new tools and opportunities for creative professionals, it also raises important questions about the role of creativity in a rapidly changing world. By embracing AI as a tool for enhancing creativity, creative professionals can ensure that their work remains unique, original, and valuable in an increasingly AI-driven world.

# CHAPTER TWENTY-SIX

# Shaping the Future of AI and Creativity

*AI and creativity are not opposing forces. They can work together to achieve new heights of innovation.*

*-   Demis Hassabis*

As the integration of AI into various industries and sectors continues to accelerate, it is important to consider the impact that these technologies will have on creativity. Industry experts have weighed in on the topic, offering unique perspectives on the future of AI and creativity.

Elon Musk, the CEO of Tesla and SpaceX, believes that AI has the potential to augment human creativity in profound ways. In an interview, he stated, "I think that AI will be the best or worst thing ever for humanity, so we need to be very careful." Musk believes that AI has the potential to enhance human creativity by allowing us to better understand complex data and systems, but that it also has the potential to limit human creativity if it is not properly regulated and controlled.

AI has the potential to be one of the greatest tools in our history for improving people's lives and making the world a better place

Similarly, Sundar Pichai, the CEO of Google, has also expressed optimism about the potential of AI to enhance human creativity. In an interview, he stated, "AI has the potential to be one of the greatest tools in our history for improving people's lives and making the world a better place." Pichai believes that AI can help humans by automating repetitive tasks, freeing up time and energy for more creative pursuits. He also stressed the importance of responsible AI development and deployment, stating that, "We have a big responsibility to ensure that AI is used ethically and for the benefit of all."

These industry leaders highlight the potential of AI to enhance human creativity, but also emphasize the importance of responsible development and deployment of these technologies. As the integration of AI continues, it is critical that we carefully consider its impact on creativity and work to ensure that it is used in ways that are beneficial to society as a whole.

*AI is a new creative medium that has the power to transform the way we express ourselves and the way we think about art and creativity.*

> *- Anna Ridler, artist and researcher.*

> *-*

The future of AI and creativity is uncertain, but the perspectives of industry leaders like Elon Musk and Sundar Pichai suggest that AI has the potential to greatly enhance human creativity, but only if it is developed and deployed responsibly. It is up to us to shape this future in a way that benefits society as a whole and allows us to harness the full potential of these powerful technologies.

# CHAPTER TWENTY-SEVEN

# DA Tales of AI - 7

## Finding a Human Touch in a World of AI

Once upon a time, in a far-off kingdom, there was a little engine named Timmy. Timmy lived in a magical world where machines and computers were everywhere, and they were changing the way things were done. Timmy was a curious little engine, and he was fascinated by the changes that were taking place.

One day, Timmy decided to set out on a journey to discover what the future of AI and creativity held. He had heard many tales of powerful machines and algorithms that could do amazing things, but he also knew that some people were worried about what the future held. Timmy wanted to see for himself and learn more about the impact of AI on creativity.

As Timmy travelled through the kingdom, he met many experts. The experts had different opinions on the future of

AI and creativity. Some believed that AI would take over the world and leave humans with nothing to do, while others believed that AI would be a powerful tool that would help humans to create and innovate like never before.

Timmy was most struck by the words of Elon Musk, the famous inventor and entrepreneur. Elon believed that AI was a double-edged sword, and that it could be both incredibly helpful and incredibly dangerous. He warned that we needed to be careful about how we developed and used AI, and that we needed to ensure that we always kept a human touch in our creative endeavours.

At the same time, Timmy also heard from Sundar Pichai, the CEO of Google. Sundar saw a bright future for AI and creativity, and he believed that AI would be a critical tool for solving some of the world's biggest problems. He encouraged Timmy to embrace the changes that were taking place, and to work hard to find ways to harness the power of AI for good.

Timmy took all of these opinions to heart, and he continued on his journey with a sense of wonder and excitement. As he travelled further, he realized that the future of AI and creativity was not a foregone conclusion, but rather a question of how we choose to shape it. He realized that it was up to all of us to work together to ensure that AI and creativity were used in ways that benefitted everyone.

And so, Timmy the little engine returned home with a sense of purpose, determined to play his part in shaping the future of AI and creativity. He continued to learn and explore, always with an eye to the future, and he remained confident that, with the right approach, AI and creativity could be a powerful force for good in the world.

# CHAPTER TWENTY-EIGHT

# Summary of Main Points

In this book, we have explored the relationship between AI and creativity and how the two are shaping the future of the creative industry. We have seen that AI is transforming the way creative work is done, from conception to execution. AI is being used to generate ideas, design products and services, and even produce final outputs like music and videos.

However, with the rise of AI, there are also concerns about its impact on the creative workforce. AI has the potential to automate many jobs and disrupt traditional ways of working, leading to job losses and changes in the skill sets required for the creative industry.

To overcome these challenges, we need to embrace AI as a tool to enhance and augment human creativity, rather than replace it. This requires a fundamental shift in the way we view AI, from a threat to an opportunity. We also need to invest in reskilling and upskilling programs to equip creative professionals with the skills they need to thrive in an AI-driven world.

We have seen that competition in the creative industry is becoming increasingly intense, and those who can harness AI to their advantage are likely to emerge as winners. However, AI is not just about replacing human creativity but also about augmenting it and enabling us to achieve outcomes that were previously beyond our reach.

In conclusion, AI is transforming the creative industry in ways that we cannot yet fully comprehend. As we move into the future, it is essential that we remain vigilant and proactive in shaping the future of AI and creativity in a way that benefits all stakeholders. As Elon Musk stated, "AI is a fundamental existential risk for human civilization and I don't think people fully appreciate that."

Similarly, Sundar Pichai, CEO of Google, has stated, "AI is going to play a big role in the future. It's going to transform every industry, every sector." It is clear that AI is going to have a significant impact on the future of creativity, and it is up to us to shape this impact in a positive way.

# CHAPTER TWENTY-NINE

# BONUS Chapter - AGI

AGI stands for Artificial General Intelligence and it refers to a type of AI that has the capability to understand or learn any intellectual task that a human being can.

Think of AGI as your friend who can not only tell jokes but also play chess, solve calculus problems and cook a gourmet meal, just like you! But unlike you, they can do all these tasks at superhuman speed and accuracy. AGI is like having a super-smart and versatile best friend.

## *AI vs AGI*

AI (Artificial Intelligence) and AGI (Artificial General Intelligence) are both forms of computer intelligence, but they differ in their capabilities.

AI is focused on performing specific tasks and is programmed to do so. For example, a virtual assistant that can answer questions or a recommendation system that suggests products based on your past purchases.

AGI, on the other hand, is a more advanced form of AI that has the ability to understand and learn any intellectual task that a human being can, not just a specific set of tasks. It has the ability to adapt and improve its performance across a wide range of tasks, just like a human being.

In short, AI is like a computer that is trained to do a specific job, while AGI is like a computer that can do any job, just like a human being.

Examples of AGI technology are still in the developmental stage, but some ongoing research projects include:

1. Neural networks and deep learning models that can learn and improve their performance over time

2. Robotics and autonomous systems that can perform a variety of tasks

3. Natural language processing models that can understand and respond to human speech

165

4. General problem-solving systems that can solve a range of problems in various domains

Some tools that are commonly used in AGI research include:

1. TensorFlow, an open-source software library for machine learning

2. PyTorch, another open-source machine learning library

3. Keras, a high-level neural network API that can be used with TensorFlow or PyTorch

4. OpenAI GPT, a language model that can generate human-like text

It is worth noting that AGI is still a very active area of research and development, and these examples and tools are likely to change and evolve rapidly in the coming years.

### *AGI as a threat*

AGI, just like any advanced technology, has the potential to pose a threat to society if not developed, used, and regulated responsibly. Some of the ways in which AGI could pose a threat include:

**Job Automation:** AGI has the potential to automate many jobs, which could result in significant job loss and unemployment for certain professions. For example, AGI could replace human workers in fields such as customer service, data entry, and repetitive manual tasks.

**Bias and Discrimination:** AGI systems can perpetuate and amplify existing biases in society if they are trained on biased data. This could lead to discrimination and unfair treatment of certain groups of people.

**Security and Privacy:** As AGI becomes more advanced, it could potentially be used to hack into systems, steal sensitive information, or cause other types of cyber-attacks.

**Ethical Concerns:** AGI raises a number of ethical concerns, such as the question of whether AGI systems should have rights, and who would be held responsible if AGI systems cause harm.

That being said, AGI also has the potential to bring about many benefits for society, such as improving medical diagnosis and treatment, increasing efficiency and productivity, and solving complex problems that humans cannot solve alone.

It's important to continue researching and developing AGI in a responsible and ethical manner to ensure that its potential benefits outweigh its potential risks.

CHAPTER THIRTY

# DA Bonus Tale of AGI- 1

### AGI Meets Fairytale: The Cinderella Story

In a kingdom far, far away, there was a beautiful young girl named Cinderella. She lived with her wicked stepmother and stepsisters who treated her poorly and made her do all the household chores.

One day, the King of the kingdom announced a ball where all eligible maidens were invited to attend and possibly win the heart of the prince. Cinderella was eager to go to the ball, but her stepmother refused to let her go.

Desperate to attend the ball, Cinderella turned to her fairy godmother for help. The fairy godmother agreed to help her and waved her wand to transform a pumpkin into a magnificent carriage and mice into horses. She also transformed Cinderella's ragged dress into a stunning ball gown.

As Cinderella was about to leave for the ball, the fairy godmother warned her that the spell would only last until midnight and that she must return before the clock strikes twelve. Cinderella agreed and went to the ball.

Meanwhile, back in the kingdom, the King and the prince were trying to find a suitable bride. They decided to use an AI system to help them in their search. The AI system was programmed to analyze the eligible maidens' characteristics and behaviors and recommend the best match for the prince.

However, when Cinderella arrived at the ball, the AI system was unable to recognize her true beauty and worth. It only saw her as a household servant and did not recommend her to the prince.

Thankfully, the prince was able to see beyond Cinderella's rough exterior and was smitten by her grace, intelligence, and kindness. He asked her to dance and they fell in love.

The prince then realized that the AI system was not enough to find his true love. He needed a more advanced form of intelligence, one that could understand and learn any intellectual task that a human being could. He needed AGI.

And so, the prince went on a quest to find AGI and eventually found Cinderella, who was the perfect match for him. They lived happily ever after, proving that AGI is a more advanced and versatile form of intelligence compared to AI.

the story of Cinderella highlights the difference between AI and AGI. AI is a type of computer intelligence that is programmed to perform specific tasks, such as analyzing eligible maidens' characteristics and behaviors. On the other hand, AGI is a more advanced form of intelligence that has the ability to understand and learn any intellectual task that a human being can, such as recognizing Cinderella's true beauty and worth.

Just like the prince needed AGI to find his true love, in our world, we may also need AGI to solve more complex and challenging problems that traditional AI systems are unable to handle.

So, the next time you hear about AI and AGI, just remember the story of Cinderella and the prince and the differ

www.ingramcontent.com/pod-product-compliance
Lightning Source LLC
La Vergne TN
LVHW051337050326
832903LV00031B/3601